RICHMOND UPON-THAMES THEN & NOW

IN COLOUR

PAUL HOWARD LANG

The History Press

This book is dedicated to my mother-in-law, Jill Whiteside, who was born and brought up in Petersham. Her reminiscences were of great help.

First published in 2013

The History Press
The Mill, Brimscombe Port
Stroud, Gloucestershire, GL5 2QG
www.thehistorypress.co.uk

© Paul Howard Lang, 2013

The right of Paul Howard Lang to be identified as the Author
of this work has been asserted in accordance with the
Copyright, Designs and Patents Act 1988.

British Library Cataloguing in Publication Data.
A catalogue record for this book is available from the British Library.

ISBN 978 0 7524 8722 9

Typesetting and origination by The History Press
Printed in India.

CONTENTS

INTRODUCTION

Originally known as Sheen, Richmond was renamed Richmond in the early sixteenth century when Henry VII built a palace here and subsequently named it after his favourite Yorkshire property, Richmond Castle. In 1849, it became a parish in its own right and became independent from Kingston-upon-Thames. Richmond was incorporated by Royal Charter in 1890, and Richmond's boundaries were enlarged in 1892 to include the parishes of Kew, Petersham and a portion of Mortlake. The area amounted to approximately 2,532 acres and of these, 1,256 are in the parish of Richmond.

Richmond was known by the sobriquet of 'Queen of the Suburbs' in 1892, before Ealing adopted the title in 1902. In 1911, the population of Richmond was 33,426, whereas the 2011 census puts the population of Richmond at 187,000.

Prior to the Victorian period, roads in Central London were not very reliable and sometimes even impassable. Traditionally, the river was used as a means of transportation, and in the nineteenth century one form of transport was the steam boat. There were horse-drawn buses but it was not until the advent of the railways that things radically changed. In July 1846, Richmond station was built, extending the London and South Western Railway line from Waterloo to Richmond, then, in 1877, from Mansion House to Richmond. By 1919, a first class single ticket from Richmond to Waterloo cost 1s, second class cost 8d and third class only 6d. In contrast, at the time of writing a single fare from Richmond to Waterloo is £4.40 and a return ticket costs £7.70. The present station at Richmond dates from 1937 and is a major terminus to central London. Surprisingly, Richmond had no tramcars running within its boundaries, apart from the service to Kew. However, the London United Electric Tramways Company brought their services right up to the Richmond boundaries on three sides, specifically on the Middlesex side at Kew Bridge, the south-western side and the south-eastern side. Cycling was popular during the Edwardian period, and is still in general favour today, particularly along the extensive cycle track that runs around Richmond Park.

There are currently fifty-two state and eighteen private schools in the Borough of Richmond, including the German School in Douglas House, along Petersham Road. Education in Richmond can best be summed up by an advertisement that appeared in 1919, expounding the scholastic advantages of the area:

Richmond is particularly well provided with really high-class educational establishments, where the best general education is provided, in conjunction with careful moral and physical training. The medical officer of health for the borough has stated that the climate is especially suited to children and the low death-rate, 11 per 1,000 in 1911, bear's eloquent witness to the salubrity of the district. Sanitary conditions and water supply are both unimpeachable and the health records in all the schools excellent.

There are numerous churches in Richmond, representing various religions, some of which will be seen later on in the book. Some of these churches have now been converted into luxury flats, for example Christ Church on Kew Road.

Richmond is only eight miles from Hyde Park Corner, and for quite some time has been a magnet for people from the metropolis who wish to come and enjoy its beauty. Richmond still draws people in to stroll along the terrace or lie in the park or take river journeys and admire the fine views, particularly during the summer months. Thousands of people descend on Richmond every day to take the train to central London, arriving by bus from neighbouring areas.

For the purposes of this book, I have included Petersham because of its strong historical links with Richmond. Not only is it geographically close but it has a fascinating history in its own right, with a wealth of historical houses and a very fine old church. One only has to walk down River Lane, Sudbrook Lane or Petersham Road, near to Montrose House, to see the quality and quantity of the ancient properties in that area. Also, Petersham is purported to have the highest density of listed buildings in England.

Some of the famous people who lived in or visited Petersham included Captain Vancouver, Charles Dickens and Vincent Van Gogh, not to mention the aristocracy who lived in the area and made it into a desirable location, right up to the present day.

The river is still important to the Borough of Richmond, although now it is primarily used for purposes of pleasure rather than trade. The boathouses along the river are testament to the lightermen, watermen and boat builders who traded from Richmond in the past. I have a strong affinity with Richmond as my wife's distant relatives, the Downs, were lightermen and watermen working in the area from at least 1688, and then later on they entered into partnership with the Collins family, entering the brewing industry. They owned parts of St Helena terrace from 1834-1901, and at one stage owned the whole Terrace as well as St Helena House nearby, and numerous other properties and public houses in the area.

All the postcards and photographs in this book are from my personal collection, acquired over many years. The modern photographs have all been taken by myself.

My grateful thanks go to the following people: Nigel Gregory, Charles Jobson, Tasmin Lang, Mr and Mrs Locherer, Jonathan Oates, Mr and Mrs Parsons, and to all at Richmond Local Studies for their invaluable help, and in particular Jane and Felix.

Paul Howard Lang, 2013

GOOSE AUCTION

IN DECEMBER 1922, it was arranged for a goose to be auctioned off at the King's Head Hotel. The King's Head was originally known as the Plough, but changed its name in the eighteenth century. The proprietor of the hotel, Mr Aston, kindly gave the proceeds from the auction to the Royal Hospital, of which Queen Victoria was the patron. Situated along Kew Foot Road, the hospital had originally been a small mansion called Rosedale. Many of the locals got involved with the auction, and the photograph below is evidence of this. It shows a group of locals gathered at the back of the King's Head on the day of the auction.

AS WELL AS the goose auction, a Boxing Day regatta was planned and ladies with collecting boxes and a barrel organ went around the town to collect money. Founded in 1907 by the Middlesex Wanderers Football Club, the regatta was comprised of an enjoyable programme of river and road events. It was decided to hold the regatta on Boxing Day in Richmond and give the proceeds to charity. The regatta of 1922 was a great success and so it became an annual event. Captain Alaway was the chairman of the committee and his brother Robert was honorary secretary. Amongst the bidders for the goose was the Mayor of Richmond, the remarkably named Alderman Percy Estcourt Metzner. The auction took place in Messum's boathouse – famous for producing high quality skiffs, which were also exported abroad – while the luncheon was held at the King's Head, at which Mr Craig proposed 'Success to the Richmond Boxing Day Regatta.'

RICHMOND BRIDGE

RICHMOND BRIDGE DATES back to 1777 and is
the only remaining Georgian bridge that crosses
the Thames. Henry Hobart laid the first stone of
the bridge and a copper plate was commissioned to
record the event, which read: 'The First Stone Of
This Bridge Was Laid By The Hon. Henry Hobart,
On The 23rd Of August Anno Domini 1774, And
In The 14th Year Of The Reign Of His Majesty
King George The Third'. James Paine designed the
bridge, along with the bridges at Kew, Chertsey and
Walton. The bridge became toll free in 1859, and
the alcoves on the side of the bridge denote where
the former tollbooths stood. In 1937, the widening
and strengthening of the bridge was undertaken
by The Cleveland Bridge and Engineering Co., Ltd.
and work was completed in the same year as the
outbreak of the Second World War, in 1939. Also
showing Tower House, built in 1856, and the

boathouses near the bridge, the older photograph (above) emphasises the importance of the river in the past. The bridge is now Grade I listed. The river brought trade and tourism to the area and in doing so turned Richmond into a prosperous town.

UNFORTUNATELY THERE IS no longer access to the Twickenham bank, as it is now private land. However, apart from the well-designed Quinlan Terry development (the buildings lining the river-front, and the terraced area) you will notice that not much else has changed; Tower House and the boathouses are still recognisable and, even with the modern development, overall this waterfront has retained its identity.

THE THAMES FROM RICHMOND BRIDGE

DATING FROM 1905, this postcard of the Thames (below) shows how popular boating was during the Edwardian period. Facing the camera on the right the White Cross Tavern can be seen, which dates back to the eighteenth century and is thought to have been built

on the site of the House of the Observant Friars. Surprisingly, the White Cross Tavern is the only public house of any real historical interest on the riverbank in Richmond. It was rebuilt in the 1830s and was once owned by the Downs family. It was also the meeting place for the Richmond Yacht Club in the Edwardian period. Mail for the club would be sent to the secretary at this tavern or to the Three Pigeon's public house, originally known as the Pigeon's Hotel, situated out of shot further along the towpath, past Richmond Bridge (see pp. 20-1).

APART FROM THE jetty, the scene today has changed remarkably little. Trees rather obscure the White Cross, but boating activity is still prevalent. A train can be seen crossing the bridge in the distance, and people still enjoy a leisurely stroll up and down the towpath.

CASTLE HOTEL

THIS UNIQUE PHOTOGRAPH was taken by the author's wife's great-grandfather, Henry Lomas, and shows the Castle Hotel taken from the river, with the White Cross Tavern on the left-hand side of the view and the bottom of Water Lane. Castle Hotel started life as a tavern in a gabled house during the reign of Charles I, and in the eighteenth century was patronised by the poet James Thompson. It moved to the site of the Assembly Rooms in the Victorian period.

The locals are lined up along the towpath watching the regatta taking place on the river. If you look carefully at the awnings on the right, you can just make out the signs for Redknap & Sons, a boat firm. In 1911, Henry William Redknap was one of a number of Redknaps working in the area. His son, Horace William, was apprenticed to him between 1906 and 1913. It was quite common for an apprenticeship to take seven years and in some cases longer. The crane on the quayside shows that even during this period, large cargoes needed to be unloaded. At this time, the river was still used as a highway for transportation of goods such as coal and timber.

THE ONLY BUILDING apart from the White Cross Tavern that corresponds with the Edwardian view is the building called Riverside House that is now a Slug and Lettuce public house, just past Water Lane. The two towers that can be seen on the roof of Riverside House in the middle of the old photograph have also gone. They belonged to Richmond Borough Water Works.

REGATTA

THE PHOTOGRAPH BELOW of a regatta was taken by Henry Lomas, who is believed to have at one time been the secretary of the Richmond Yacht Club. Regattas were extremely popular in the Edwardian period, as the vast number of peole watcing the event in this photograph shows. Note the people standing on the original Richmond railway bridge, which was built in 1848 and made of cast iron. It was designed by Joseph Locke and John

Errington, and the contractor was Thomas Brassey. The bridge was replaced in 1908 by a steel one, to the same design as its predecessor. This newer version was designed by J.W. Jacomb Hood, and the arches had a span of 100ft. The railway first came to Richmond in 1846, and in 1877 the Metropolitan District Railway, which later became the District line, would vastly increase the number of people travelling into Richmond.

TODAY, THE SCENE is remarkably similar; except for the lack of boats. Beyond the railway bridge in the foreground, Twickenham Bridge can be seen, which was designed by Alfred Dryland and built in 1933. The bridge in the background is Richmond lock and weir footbridge, which dates back to 1894 and was opened by the Duke and Duchess of York.

ST HELENA TERRACE

NAMED AFTER THE island Napoleon was exiled to in 1815, St Helena Terrace was, as it is now, a popular place to take a stroll. On the left-hand side of the old photograph (right), it is just possible to make out some of the boathouses which still grace the side of the river today. This is a very good view of the sailing craft, and the charming image of the young girl looking out across the river truly reflects those halcyon days by the river.

THERE ARE FEW notable changes in today's image of St Helena Terrace. The road surface has now been cobbled, but there is still vegetation growing along the side of the river bank. People still like to promenade along the riverfront, boats can be seen in the distance, and Richmond Bridge is still visible. However, the trees have obscured the view of Tower House, which dates to 1856, and the other buildings near the bridge on the left. The White Cross public house can be clearly seen to the left with the name visible above the boathouses.

THE RIVER
TOWARDS PETERSHAM

BY THE AMOUNT of activity on the riverside, it would seem that this old photograph is
depicting the moments before a regatta race. This lively view of the river, looking towards
Petersham, shows the towpath thronging with people. Boating was an extremely
popular pastime, and this image shows how the river attracted large numbers of people.
Hiring boats was very popular at this time, as can be seen by the amount of boats for hire
on the water.

IN THE MODERN scene we see only moored boats, no craft actually being sailed, and in stark contrast to the older image there are only a few people strolling along the river bank. The trees appear to have been tamed slightly, and the steps leading up to a lawned area are clearly visible.

19

PIGEON'S HOTEL

ALTHOUGH THIS POSTCARD is labelled Pigeon's Hotel, the emphasis of the view is clearly on the more dominant boathouse building. This boathouse was the home of Messums & Sons, boatbuilders and watermen renowned for their well-built skiffs, which were even exported abroad. The rowing boats enliven the picture and the parasol adds to the leisurely aspect of the scene. You can also see the launching ramps for the boats and the row of boathouses in the left of the image. In 1912, the landlord of the Pigeon's Hotel was William Giles East, and later the name of the pub was changed to The Raj. However, a fire destroyed a lot of the building in 1994 and it closed as a public house.

NEXT TO THE building that was once the Pigeon's Hotel, some luxurious flats were built over the boathouse. The boathouse next to the flats now houses the Richmond Canoe Club, which was established in 1944.

RICHMOND
TERRACE GARDENS

THE TERRACE GARDENS command a spectacular view of the Thames, showing the river's majestic curve set amongst a panorama of unspoilt nature. The view from Richmond Hill was so highly regarded that it has been protected by the Richmond, Petersham and Ham Open Spaces Act of 1902, and is famous for being one of the finest river views in England. Many postcards of Richmond feature the Terrace Gardens, but this one struck me as being particularly beautiful, with the river being framed by the trees. The American William Byrd (1674-1744) was so inspired by the view of the Thames from the Terrace, that he named a new city in the USA, founded on the James River in Virginia, as Richmond, in 1737.

TODAY'S IMAGE SHOWS a similar view, however, the season has changed, the trees are lusher and the small island on the river is more visible. The sea of trees on the opposite bank show what an unspoilt spot this is, and one can immediately see what attracts people to this idyllic area.

TOWER HOUSE

MORE LIKE A miniature piece of art work, this charming artist's impression of the steps leading to Richmond Bridge has a very Mediterranean feel to it, possibly because of Tower House on the left, which is very Italianate in character. Dating to 1856, Tower House was built by a local builder named Long, to the design of Henry Laxton. Laxton was the brother of Wililam Laxton, who was famous for *The Builders' Price Book* – a standard work in the building profession. This postcard was produced by Raphael Tuck, who conceived some really aesthetically pleasing cards. The insert in the picture depicts a finely-dressed waterman, who would have plied his trade along the waterfront, looking for important clients to transport on the river.

TODAY, TOWER HOUSE has hardly changed at all. Although there are no people using the steps in the modern photograph, they are still extremely popular, with people going up and down them all the time. It appears that the only difference between then and now is the old handrail on the left (seen in the artist's impression), which has now gone.

Steps
Richm

THE TERRACE

WITH THE DISTINGUISHED houses on the right, this beautifully evocative card dates back to 1904 and shows people sitting down on the benches along The Terrace and admiring the view. During the Edwardian period, this was a rather fashionable area to promenade. The view of the grand houses on the right is slightly blocked by the overhanging trees. On a really clear day, Windsor and up to six more counties can be seen from the vantage point of The Terrace. In regard to the fine houses on the Terrace, No. 1 was built around 1700 by Michael Pew and No. 3 was purchased by William Hickey in 1700. Mrs Fitzherbert was also

purported to have lived at No. 3 when she first met the Prince of Wales, the future George IV. Mrs Fitzherbert was widowed for the second time in 1781 and moved to Richmond; she eventually agreed to marry him, but it was a morganatic marriage. They were married in the drawing room of her London house and possibly honeymooned in Richmond.

THE MODERN VIEW of The Terrace is, sadly, dominated by parked cars, however, people can still be seen walking along The Terrace, enjoying the wide open space along the river. Strangely, in contrast to the older image, no one is sitting on the benches.

TERRACE WALK

THE POSTCARD BELOW is dated 1948 and shows the curved part of Terrace Walk. A group of people can be seen walking along the terrace, and the Park Gate Hotel is just visible on the right of the image. The hotel, just past Friars Style Road, was known as the Mount View Hotel from 1933 onwards, until it was renamed the Mount Royal Hotel from 1940-48.

THE RAILINGS AND posts were replaced to mark the Queen's Silver Jubilee in 1977, the design being kept as near as possible to the original, and even though the ubiquitous motor car now dominates the road, the former Park Gate Hotel is still recognisable. On

Friars Style Road, opposite the hotel, the house on the corner has been demolished and Hillbrow, a block of upmarket flats, has taken its place. Note the number of parked cars in the modern scene.

THE DUCHESS OF TECK MEMORIAL

TAKEN IN 1930, this image (right) shows a memorial, built in 1891, that commemorates the Duchess of Teck's association with the town. The Duchess of Teck lived at White Lodge in Richmond Park. Her father, Prince Adolphus, the Duke of Cambridge, was the youngest surviving son of George III. The Duchess of Teck was the current Queen's great-grandmother. The memorial is constructed in the Art Nouveau style; it is inscribed with the following words: 'Erected by the Richmond branch of the Royal Society for the Preservation of Cruelty

to Animals'. The dragons at the top of this monument are very distinctive, as are the lamps on the corners and it makes for an impressive landmark at the top of Richmond Hill. Notice the two men on the roof of the Morshead Hotel painting the side of the building.

THE ROAD MARKINGS rather spoil the current view, and note that the water has gone from the bottom part of the monument, having been replaced by some brightly coloured annuals. The top cylindrical part of the fountain has also disappeared. The hotel is still recognisable, apart from the now-missing chimney pots on the roof.

PETERSHAM ROAD

THE ROAD THAT connected Richmond with Petersham was a very ancient roadway, and can be traced back to the sixteenth century. It consisted of a road over the hill and a lower road, and it is Lower Road, as it was called, which was renamed Petersham Road in 1893. This postcard of the Petersham Road (right), near the junction to Star and Garter Hill, dates to 1904. A wagon can be seen on the left of the scene and the man appears to be checking the wheel. A man on a horse has stopped, presumably to have his photo taken, and a very smartly dressed gentleman in a top hat is looking directly at the camera. The scene has been taken at the edge of

Petersham Common Woods; land which was originally part of Ham House estate, but was donated by the 9th Earl of Dysart in 1900, when Richmond Council gained the freehold of the common.

THE SLIGHT CURVE to the road is still recognisable today. However, the old signpost has gone and a low fence now defines the path into the woods. Even though this looks like a quiet spot, the traffic can be quite considerable, particularly during rush hour. It is no longer the remote area that it appears in the old card; although even this picture suggests that there was a regular flow of traffic along the Petersham Road towards Richmond itself. Petersham Common Conservators have now taken over the management of the common, and it has some fine old trees and a wealth of plants. It is still popular with walkers and is a relatively unspoilt area that has retained a lot of its original beauty.

GEORGE STREET

GEORGE STREET IS the oldest street in Richmond and named after George III, who had a palace at Kew. The most prominent shop seen in this early postcard view is that of the Wright Brothers drapers' store, first opened in 1877 by Arthur and Frederick Wright. One can also spot on the right-hand side Lilley and Skinner Ltd, the boot makers, and the Lipton grocery store next door, showing what a diverse shopping area George Street had become by the Edwardian era. A variety of horse-drawn vehicles can be seen parked along the sides of the street, as well as people walking along the pavement.

TODAY, THE OLD Wright Brothers store has gone and a Tesco Metro store has taken its place. However, the building above the shop is still recognisable, as is the double-bowed frontage above Lilley and Skinner. George Street is still a busy shopping street.

GEORGE STREET (TOWARDS THE QUADRANT)

THIS INCREDIBLE IMAGE of George Street looking towards the Quadrant and railway station (below) is superb in its depiction of the shops, people and transport of the early twentieth century. On the left-hand side of the road there is the London, City and Midland Bank, the manager in 1905 being Mr G. Pollard. The City and Midland Bank was known as the Midland Bank in 1836, then, in 1891, it acquired Central Bank of London, then in 1898

bought The City Bank, hence its name at the time. Next door to the bank was Abbotts & Sons, the boot manufacturers. Further down the street was the London and South West Bank. Beyond Brewer's Lane can be seen the Wright Brothers drapers' shop, in the building which is slightly projected. Kempthorne and Phillips, another drapers, can be seen on the right of the image, and just beyond that, past Victoria Place, the sign for the Greyhound Hotel. This hotel was also used for property auctions, in particular by Nightingale Chancellors estate agents, which was started during George III's reign. They had premises at No. 1 King Street which dated to 1807. The chimney in the middle distance was owned by the Electric Light Company, but was dismantled in 1914.

TODAY'S VIEW BEARS little resemblance to the old one. The shops have all radically changed in the modern photograph, and the only recognisable building is the former Wright Brothers premises, where one can still distinguish the side windows and chimney stacks.

HILL STREET

HILL STREET IS so named as it leads to Richmond Hill. The part from Bridge Street to Heron Court was once called Royal Terrace, and from Heron Court up to Town Hill was once called Clarence Terrace. Hill Street can be traced back to 1770, and Richmond Theatre used to stand in this street. This postcard shows Hill Street around the time of the First World War – notice the soldier walking along the pavement on the left. Bensted's music warehouse can be seen on the right-hand side of the road, of which there was also a branch in Ealing Broadway, and you can see the sign for the Ladies Tea Rooms next to Bensted's. Some interesting forms of transport can also be seen in this view; the horse-drawn cart looks extremely well laden with wooden boxes.

BENSTED'S CLOSED DOWN in 1957 due to ill health of the managing director, Montagu Adams. Bensted's had been established in Hill Street for over 100 years, before it was eventually purchased by Richard and Partners Properties Ltd. The old Town Hall can be seen in the old picture on the left, with the clock on top. The Town Hall was built in the 1890s on land donated by Sir John Whittaker Ellis, who was the first mayor for the new Borough of Richmond. It moved in the 1960s as a new Civic Centre was built in Twickenham. The old Town Hall building now houses the Reference Department of the Library, Local Studies, and Richmond Museum.

HILL STREET, 1904

THIS IS A stunning image of Richmond in 1904, showing people shopping along Hill Street. A very clear view can be seen of the Royal Arms, the proprietor of which, at this time, was Percy Wheeler. Next door to that, on the left, was Dixey & Co. Opticians; note the eye chart in the window. Also notice the sign for W.J. Byrne & Co. photographers near the pillar box. In 1880, Byrne & Co. charged 15s for a large portrait measuring 18x8 inches. During the Edwardian period, photography became very popular and people would go to the photographers to have their portrait taken, and also photographs that marked the milestones in life such as, weddings, anniversaries and births. Byrne & Co. were photographers and miniature painters to the Queen, and were established in 1883 and continued till 1910. The other rival photographers were George Tuohy, established in 1870 at No. 2, The Quadrant. Beyond Whittaker Avenue, which runs alongside the Town Hall (the building

with the clock), you can see another public house, the Spread Eagle, of which Mr Dooley was the proprietor. The amount of detail that can be seen in this card is incredible and really gives a good impression of what life was like during this period.

IN TODAY'S PHOTOGRAPH, all the lovely old shops and the pub have gone and modern development has taken their place, and there now stands tall corporate-looking buildings. The old Town Hall clock, however, is still in place today, as are the buildings to the left of it.

HILL STREET, 1920s

THIS IS A remarkably detailed
street scene from the 1920s.
Although labelled High Street,
this is in fact Hill Street, shown
from just beyond Whittaker
Avenue looking towards
Ormond Road. Note the
projected canopy with the glass
sign for Ellis & Co. on the right
of the image. Established in
1836, Ellis & Co. were wine and
spirit merchants; hence the
sign outside for Scotch
whisky for 12s and 6d. Ellis
& Co. was a long-established
firm and also had a branch
at No. 56 Friars Stile Road.
A very old grapevine once

grew over the roof canopy of the wine merchants in Hill Street, having been planted in 1840. The street named The Vineyard, off Hill Rise, recalls the days when grapes were successfully grown in Richmond. Ellis & Co. finally moved from Richmond after 141 years, to a building named Richmond House in Sheerwater, near Woking, in 1970. The National Provincial Bank can be seen next door, which was established in 1833, but is no longer in business.

YOU CAN STILL recognise the view by the layout of the windows above the shops on the left, but the shops themselves have entirely changed; All Bar One now stands where Ellis & Co. once was.

BRIDGE STREET

BRIDGE STREET WAS originally called Ferry Hill, due to the ferry that used to operate from this riverside position, well before Richmond Bridge was constructed. The name Ferry Hill can be traced back to the year 1604. Bridge Street held a diverse range of shops and was a popular area in Richmond for people to come shopping; the bridge is teeming with people crossing in both directions. Notice the sign for the superbly named Ye Dainties Luncheon and Tea Rooms. Next to Ye Dainties was Gaynor & Sons, a fishing tackle and sporting goods store, and Pavey's, a frame making shop. Further down the road was Elite, an art needlework establishment, which was next to a milliners shop. On the other side of the road was Bridge House, a residential hotel, whose proprietor at the time was Mr Beare. Bridge House was designed by Robert Taylor, who was knighted

in 1783. In his later life he served as Vice President on the Board of the Foundling Hospital in London. Bridge House was once occupied by Viscount Ranelagh, and also by Major Martin and Edward Martin in 1853. The tower past the row of shops on the right is Tower House (see pp.24-5).

ONE MAJOR DIFFERENCE between the two images is that it would be unwise nowadays to stand in the middle of the road, as the young boy is doing in the Edwardian scene. A van is now in the spot where the horse and cart stood in the old image.

THE QUADRANT

THERE ARE SEVERAL interpretations of the origins of the name The Quadrant, a likely one being that it was the road that leads from The Square. This area of Richmond was at one time known as World's End, as the town gate was sited here. It was not until 1876 that The Quadrant, as we know it today, was built. This picture highlights how busy the area along The Quadrant was, even during the early twentieth century. Note the interesting artefacts in the Hunt & Co. shop on the left. It would seem that the people in the street are still not used to having their photograph taken; look at how the lady with the

pram has stopped and turned her head towards the camera. The cart with its stacked wicker baskets, on the right of the image, is another interesting focal point, and the Brown Bear public house is very dominant in the scene, with its Watney, Coombe & Reid (the brewery company) sign at the top of the building.

ALTHOUGH THE SHOPS have all changed and the Brown Bear has gone, the scene is still recognisable today. The roof line on the left of the image is unchanged; the rows of dormer windows and the windows below are still the same, although the awnings are a thing of the past.

RICHMOND HILL AND PETERSHAM ROAD

DATING FROM 1924, this postcard shows what a busy area this part of Richmond was. On the right, people can be seen looking into one of the shop windows. Notice the sign for the Cosy Corner tea rooms, the prominent sign for Law's British Toy Shop and the Holbrook Motor Company's garage. Petersham Road was very narrow at this period, and the No. 73 bus is forced to wait for another oncoming bus to come through.

A superb old lamp post junction divides the two roads. Out of sight, down the right-hand fork in the road, just on the left was the Poppy factory. It was established in 1922, but moved in 1925 to its new location, the disused Richmond Brewery Stores on Petersham Road. In 1933, the factory was rebuilt, and now produces approximately 36 million poppies and 80,000 poppy wreaths each year.

TODAY'S PHOTOGRAPH SHOWS that the road has now been widened, and it is evident that the area continues to be a popular place to frequent. The buildings have gone in the triangle between the two roads and have been replaced by a green space, and iron bollards have been placed along the edges of the roads. The Tea Rooms have been replaced with Café Paolo, reflecting the public's change in tastes.

PETERSHAM
BEND IN THE ROAD

DATING FROM AROUND 1928, the image below highlights how rural Petersham was at the time. On the right is Myrtle Cottage, which is still standing today, however, the iron railings along the front have gone. An old bollard can be seen in front of the alley leading to Sudbrook Lane, which separates Myrtle Cottage from its neighbour, Rosedale House. Just beyond this were some outbuildings that were reputed to be haunted. On the left, the white building was the original Fox and Hound public house.

ALTHOUGH THE ROAD looks free of traffic, I had to wait a considerable time for a break in the flow to capture this shot. Myrtle Cottage can still be seen on the right and Rosedale House is unchanged, apart from the TV aerial on the roof. The bollard has gone and a tall streetlamp has taken its place. The outbuildings have also disappeared and the new Fox and Duck has been built closer to Rosedale House than it previously was. Despite these changes, the scene is still recognisable, with the sweeping bend in the road to the left of the picture.

PETERSHAM ROAD TOWARDS HAM

THE EARL OF Dysart sold off plots of land along Petersham Road in around 1927, and houses were built from the Richmond end going back towards Ham. You will notice that there is a gap between the end of the 1920s buildings and the Victorian cottage on the left, and that the cottages were on a slightly different alignment to the 1920s houses.

The house just before the gap is No. 203 Petersham Road. Number 201, which is just visible, was originally called 'Stowe' before numbers were introduced.
Also, notice the extension at the side of the Victorian cottage.

TODAY'S VIEW SHOWS that the long wooden fences have gone and driveways have been opened up for the residents to park their cars. The trees and shrubs greatly enhance the properties, which is now a conservation area.

PETERSHAM ROAD

THIS UNIQUE PHOTOGRAPH
of Petersham Road was taken
in 1932 by Samuel Eaton, my
wife's grandfather. It shows how
quiet the road was during this
period; only one vehicle can be
seen. The large house opposite,
now called Whornes Place, is very
distinctive. During the Second
World War, an incendiary device
fell on the roof of the house,
which the photographer helped to
put out. Also, it seems that wooden
fencing was extremely fashionable
during this era; nearly every
property is surrounded by it.

IN CONTRAST, TODAY'S image shows that the long wooden fences have gone and brick walls have taken their place. The traffic along Petersham Road has vastly increased, as it is now a major route into Richmond in one direction and Kingston in the other. The location of Richmond and Petersham, with the river on one side and the park on the other, makes it impossible for a bypass to be constructed. In 2011, actors Brad Pitt and Angelina Jolie rented Whornes House.

THE STAR AND GARTER HOTEL AND PETERSHAM ALMSHOUSES

THE STAR AND Garter is perhaps the most iconic building in Richmond, which has been through many incarnations. It started life as a small inn, gradually growing in size until it became a hotel, which closed in 1910. The Petersham almshouses, which are below on the

left, were originally sited further up the hill. The three arches give them a distinctive architectural feature, as do the cluster of chimney pots on the top of most of the roofs. Unfortunately, they were demolished in 1953.

THE ORIGINAL STAR and Garter was designed by E.M. Barry and looks like a French chateau. The building was requisitioned by the army during the First World War, but was demolished soon after. Today, the new Royal Star and Garter Home (as it is now known) is a home for ex-servicemen. It was built on the site of the former building in 1924 and was designed by Sir Edwin Cooper in a neo-Georgian style. It does not, however, have the grandeur of the former building. There is a luxuriant amount of trees and shrubbery surrounding the area, in refreshingly unspoilt vistas.

THE STAR AND GARTER HOTEL'S ANNEXE

LOOKING VERY DIFFERENT from the Royal Star and Garter Home that replaced this building, we see the hotel's annexe which dates to 1874. The building has a very impressive skylight, interesting chimney stacks, and the rounded arches above the windows are strong architectural features. There is a splendid old tree behind the wall on the right, and a parked carriage can be seen on the corner. Wick House, which dates to 1772, can be seen in the middle distance. Designed by Sir William Chambers, it was once the residence of the painter Sir Joshua Reynolds.

THE ROYAL STAR and Garter Home was opened in 1924 and replaced the former hotel. It was designed by Sir Edwin Cooper and was opened by George V and Queen Mary as a home for disabled servicemen. Sadly, the old tree has gone and Wick House is now hidden behind trees.

PARK GATES

RICHMOND GATE AND its lodges were built to the designs of John Soane (later knighted) between 1795 and 1798. Soane was the architect of the Bank of England building and Pitzhanger Manor in Ealing – an incredibly innovative architect of his day. A magnificent aquatint of the Park Gates by Jonathan Brown, dating to 1810, can be viewed at the Richmond Museum in the old Town Hall building. Due to the increase in road traffic, the gates had to be widened in 1896.

THERE ARE OBVIOUS signs of change in today's view, with new road markings, street furniture and parked cars. A tree partly obscures the view of the lodge on the left-hand side, but the lodge on the right can be seen much more clearly. One of the main differences between today's image and the old one is that the tall chimney structure has gone and another building has appeared behind the lodge. The drinking fountain just in front of the lodge has lost its circular feature; the inscription on this reads: 'The Princess Mary Adelaide Duchess of Teck 27th October 1897'.

THE MAIDS OF HONOUR ROW

THIS DISTINGUISHED ROW of houses was built in 1725 on the site of the old Richmond Palace and housed the ladies in waiting of the Princess of Wales, later Queen Caroline. One of the famous residents of the Maids of Honour Row was Judith Levy, a very rich but slightly eccentric lady who was extremely philanthropic and helped the people of the local area considerably.

On Sunday, 3 August 1879, there was a disastrous hail storm that broke nearly every window along the Row. A hail storm relief fund was started from the Greyhound Hotel, which received £875 from private individuals and public institutions, and was distributed by the churches in Richmond. Close to the Maids of Honour Row you can still see the iron posts and rails that bear the cipher of William IV, and also the remains of the old palace.

THE MAIDS OF Honour Row, now private residencies, still looks very impressive today, and one can tell the buildings' venerable age and respectability even from a distance. Notice, though, that two rather mature trees on either side of the path have now gone. The trees along the edge of the green remain, and partially block the view of the Maids of Honour Row.

RICHMOND THEATRE

RICHMOND THEATRE WAS opened on
18 September 1899, and the Ben Greet Company
performed the first play there, Shakespeare's
As You Like It. The theatre was originally called the
Theatre Royal and Opera House; it then became the
Richmond Hippodrome and finally Richmond Theatre.
The architect was Frank Matcham, a famous theatre
architect – Richmond Theatre is often cited as being one
of his finest creations, and a room within the theatre
bears his name in honour. This was the fifth theatre to
be built in Richmond, and is located on Little Green.
One is struck by the abundance of creeping foliage that
has colonised the sides of the building. There are a few
people walking by the theatre, and there is a distinct
lack of signs advertising forthcoming plays.

TODAY'S IMAGE SHOWS that the foliage which covered most of the left-hand side of the building has gone and there is a noticeable difference in the amount of trees in front of the building; only one tree is visible. The Barclays Bank office building has now been built next to the theatre. A new extension has been built on the right-hand side of the theatre and it now looks far more commercial.

ELLERKER COLLEGE

AN EDWARDIAN ADVERTISEMENT for Ellerker College described it as being 'For the daughters of gentlemen', and is a fine example of a school. The house, which belonged to the Houblon family, was first mentioned in 1726 but is possibly of even earlier origin. The Houblons kept the property till 1780 when it was bought by Mrs Ellerker, who resided in it until she died in 1842. The school – known as Ellerker College – was founded by Mrs Yarrow and dates from 1889 until 1931; it then became the Old Vicarage School in that year. Its castellated exterior makes it a very distinctive and attractive building, which stands out amongst the other buildings in the neighbourhood.

SADLY, THE PINNACLES have gone and some of the magic of the building has been lost with their absence. The building has been re-painted a startling white and the foliage has gone, which makes the building look clearer but less romantic. Two very prominent but necessary fire escapes now appear on the side, bollards have replaced the lamp post, and there is a TV aerial on the roof. Apart from the road markings the view is very similar, except for the railings on the side, where there had previously been a wall.

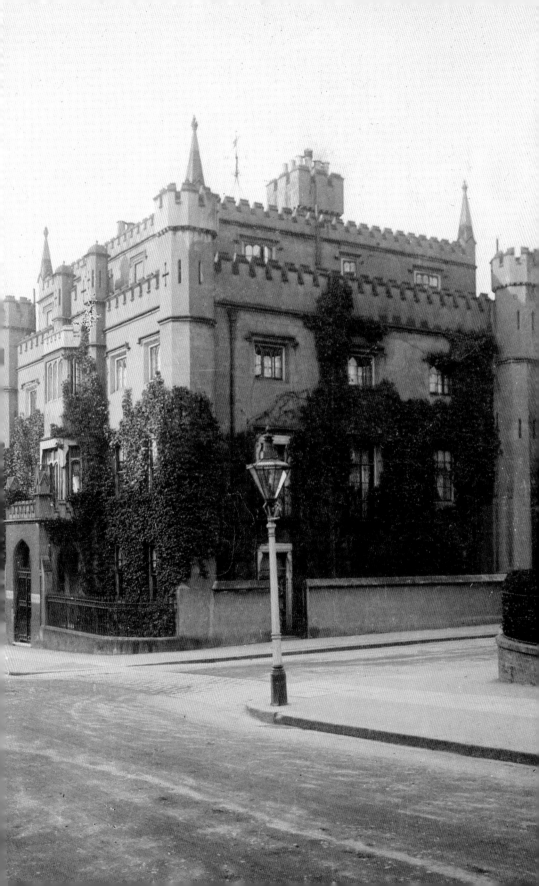

WILLIAM HICKEY'S ALMSHOUSES

WILLIAM HICKEY ASTUTELY bought some very desirable properties on Richmond Hill, which included the famous Wick House. As a result, when he died in 1727, the Trust that had been set up to administer his charitable wishes had enough capital to build the almshouses and administer them. Taken in 1950, this image (right) shows what an interesting set of buildings they were, comprised with the tall chimney stacks giving a unique architectural feature to the skyline. The almshouses date to 1834, and were designed by architect Lewis Vulliamy (1791-1871). The chapel with the step roof can be seen on the right of the image, next to the Church Estate almshouses. Between them they cover a considerable amount of land.

SILVER BIRCH TREES now obscure the buildings in the modern photograph, which are now managed by the Richmond Charities and are Grade II listed. It is clear that the lawn is still very well kept, with the addition of a bench on the lawn for recreation purposes.

ABERCORN HOUSE

ABERCORN WAS VERY distinguished
looking and one can immediately tell
that it was a house of some importance.
The house was probably completed
in 1869, and the 1880 directory
for Richmond names the occupier
as William Grahame. The exiled
King Manuel of Portugal was amongst
Abercorn's many occupants, along with
his mother, Queen Amelia, who rented it
in December 1910. The ex-King went to
live in Fulwell Park in Twickenham after
his marriage, but Queen Amelia lived at
Abercorn until 1920. It then passed to
Robert Mitchell Graham, who resided
there until 1932, when the house was
demolished. Interestingly, the private
secretary to King Manuel, the Marquis

de Lavradio, resided at a house called Erpingham, which was situated lower down King's Road, and at that time various other members of the Portuguese nobility had residencies in this vicinity.

A GROUP OF houses now stand on the two plots that originally made up Abercorn House and it is obvious that it once had a rather large garden area; one can still see the original side entrance to the garden along Chester Avenue. The house extended from Chester Avenue to Marchmont Road, and was a formidably sized property. It is possible that the original photograph of Abercorn House was taken from the Marchmont Road side, but now the wall and property have been knocked down and at the time of writing building work is taking place on this site.

ELM LODGE

ELM LODGE IN Petersham dates back to 1762. This fact alone singles it out as an outstanding building. It has remarkable historical associations – Charles Dickens, who, in 1839, rented Elm Cottage (as it was known then), wrote part of *Nicholas Nickleby* here. Dickens was also well known for entertaining his friends in the Star and Garter Hotel in Richmond, which was fairly close to Elm Lodge. During the Second World War, Elm Lodge was used as part of a network of secret locations dealing with radar, and was commandeered by the government for top secret research and training purposes, all of which remained shrouded in mystery to the inhabitants of Petersham. Not only that, but during the war, a British aeroplane crashed onto the roof of Elm Lodge. The building was not handed back over to the owners until April 1946.

TODAY, THE MOST noticeable difference is the absence of the greenhouse and the garden path, as well as the veranda awning that ran around the side of the house. Nowadays, it is a private residential house and the main entrance is no longer on Petersham Road but from Dickens Close at the rear.

RICHMOND COUNTY SCHOOL

RICHMOND COUNTY SCHOOL for Boys along Kew Road is striking in its design. Construction on the building was started in 1895 but it was not completed until 1901, when the south wing was finally built. Mr Buckhurst was the headmaster. George Cave was the Chairman of the Governors of the school, and Clifford Edgar was the Chairman of the Technical Education Committee. The foundation stone was laid by His Royal Highness the Duke of Cambridge on 24 July 1895. Railings surrounding the front of the school stopped boys from climbing in the trees. During a

particularly hot summer in 1944 many of the schools in Richmond held classes outdoors near to the air-raid shelters, so that if an attack did come the pupils would be able to seek shelter quickly. This was at the time when doodlebug bombs were falling short of London, and sometimes the children had to go to the air-raid shelters up to six times a day. Even examinations were held in the outdoors. On a more practical level, buckets filled with sand were used as makeshift toilets for the pupils.

THE SCHOOL HAS now been turned into a block of flats called Bishop Court. Some of the windows have been partially boarded over, and the trees rather obscure the view in the modern photograph.

RUSSELL
BRITISH
SCHOOL

WHEN LORD RUSSELL founded the school at Petersham
in 1849, classes were held in one room. They would
continue to do so until 1852, when a purpose-built
school was constructed in Petersham Park. In 1891,
it changed its name to the Russell British School, as
by this time it had been adopted by the British and
Foreign School Society. The different coloured roof tiles,
making the cross pattern on the roof, creates a very
striking aesthetic. This image pre-dates the First World
War; tragically, the school was destroyed by a bomb in
November 1943. I spoke to a woman who had attended
this school during the Second World War and she
informed me that when an air raid was imminent, the
children were led by the teachers from each class all the

way to the crypt of All Saints' Church. As the war progressed, an air-raid shelter was built behind the school, but unfortunately the school was bombed before it could be used.

THE SCHOOL WAS situated very close to the park gates and today these are the only link with the former building. Today, Petersham Park is a popular place for local people to visit.

OLD PALACE LANE

OLD PALACE LANE can be traced back to 1772, when an Act of Parliament was concerned with repairing and maintaining this road. Old Palace Lane is important as it links The Green to the river. During the Victorian period it was known as Asgill Lane. The White Swan public house was initially called the Asgill Arms, named after the historic Asgill House that stands by the river. Asgill House was named after Sir Charles Asgill. Before houses were numbered for the convenience of the postman, it was very common for a house to be named after its owner.

THE REGENCY COTTAGES are still recognisable in the modern photograph, but the hedges have now gone. The wall on the left is now covered in ivy and six metal bollards and a new lamp post have appeared, slightly changing the appearance of the scene.

THE FOX AND DUCK

THIS IS AN original photograph of the Fox and Duck public house taken in 1932 by my wife's grandfather, Samuel Eaton, who lived in Petersham. The Fox and Duck originally dates back to the 1730s. One's eye is immediately drawn to the tall chimney at the side of the building, and note the watchman's hut and village lock-up, which was erected in 1782, at the side of the pub. The village pound area was originally at the back of the lock-up, but was moved to the front in 1940. The area was used for keeping stray cattle until they were claimed by the local farmers or villagers. The most famous watchman employed in the hut was Richard Wigley who, in 1821, tried to stop a horse and cart driven by Robert Knight, who was smuggling spirits. In the course of his duty, Wigley fired at Knight, who subsequently died. Wigley was found guilty of manslaughter and sentenced to six months' imprisonment.

THE FOX AND Duck was rebuilt around 1940 and was re-sited slightly further away from the old lock-up. Originally called the Horse and Groom, the pub dates back to approximately 1730 and was a posting house on the stagecoach route from London to Guildford. It is sad that the fantastic tottering chimney has gone. The pub now has two straight chimneys at the front of the building, but nothing like the rather ramshackle character of the old pub. The road markings are prominent in comparison to the lovely open space in the old photograph. The block of houses behind the pub were built in 1969.

ST MARY MAGDALENE

RICHMOND'S PARISH CHURCH lies nestled between two busy roads, an oasis of peace and calm. It has some very fine memorials, the most famous being that of actor Edmund Kean, who trod the boards at Richmond Theatre, and also poet James Thomson, amongst many others. This image, dating from 1906, gives a good view of the tower, which dates from 1507, and the main body of the church, with the graveyard in front and the railings that run along Church Walk. The tower contains the church bells, of which three of the eight (which make the octave) date back to the seventeenth century, the remainder to the eighteenth century. One of the bells has a unique inscription, which reads: 'Lambert made me weake not fit to ring,

but Bartlet amongst the rest hath made me sing' – James Bartlet being the person who corrected the fault in the bell. Clearly visible is the external white monument of a woman weeping over an urn. The tablet is dedicated to the memory of Barbara Hofland, author of *The Son of a Genius*, who died in Richmond on 4 November 1844, aged seventy-four.

THE MOST NOTICEABLE change in the modern photograph is how the trees have grown up and obscured a great deal of the church. The tower cannot be seen from this angle, and the Hofland monument is obscured as well. The railings, a casualty of the Second World War, have gone and so have the gravestones, which have moved to the other side of the path. In fact, one has to look extremely hard to identify it as the same place.

ST JOHN'S CHURCH

ST JOHN'S CHURCH stands on Kew Road, not far from the railway station. It dates to 1836 and was designed by the same architect who designed Hickey's almshouses, Lewis Vulliamy. The land that St John's stood on was given by the Selwyn family, who, as major landowners, were an important local family. When the local population increased due to the coming of the railway the parish church could not accommodate everyone, so new churches were established on the periphery of the town. St John's is an example of this. The church has a beautiful gothic spire with fine pinnacles all pointing heavenward. One can only guess as to why the group of children are congregated in front of the church.

THE MOST NOTICEABLE thing in the modern view is how the tree has grown up and obscured the view. You can still see some of the beautiful pinnacles sticking up above the branches. Although this looks like a tranquil scene, the traffic roars along this road in a non-stop fury.

HOLY TRINITY CHURCH

DATING FROM THE Edwardian period, this photo was taken from Townshend Road, near Sheen Park. This Anglican church dates to 1870 and, like St John's, is quite a distance from St Mary Magdalene parish church. In 1880 the tower was added but was unfortunately knocked down in 1970. In 1913, the vicar was the Revd L.R. Hancock. No people or vehicles obstruct the view, but a solidly built wall, with a dog-tooth feature at the top, defines the church boundary, and a single lamp post stands guard outside.

AN EXTENSION HAS been added onto the side of the church where the tower used to stand. A tree partially obscures the building, but you can still recognise the main body of the church. The old wall has gone, but a newer wall has replaced it that is still in keeping with the church architecture.

ST MATTHIAS' CHURCH

THIS POSTCARD SHOWS what a beautifully proportioned spire St Matthias' has and I also like the fact that the photographer has captured the image of a boy standing in the middle of the road, which gives an indication as to the height of the spire. Note the luxuriant foliage behind the wall, partially blocking out some of the view of the church. St Matthias' Church was designed by Sir George Gilbert Scott in the gothic style. The foundation stone was laid by Charles Jasper Selwyn on 14 April 1857, and the Selwyn family donated the land on which the church stands in Friars Style Road. The building of the church was undertaken by Messrs Piper & Sons of Bishopsgate Street in London. St Matthias' Church was consecrated on 7 August 1858 by the Right Revd Charles Richard Winton, Bishop of Winchester.

THE MOST NOTICEABLE thing in the modern photograph is how the road is now dominated by parked vehicles and has lost its tranquil aspect. The distinctive roof of the building on the right remains the same.

CHRIST CHURCH, KEW ROAD

CHRIST CHURCH
WAS dedicated
on St Peter's Day,
29 June 1894. It was
built as a memorial
to the Revd Canon
J.D. Hales, who was the
vicar for forty years
at St John's Church.
It was designed by
Arthur Blomfield
in the Early English
style and could seat
750 worshippers.
The exterior walls are
constructed of Bath
stone and Kentish rag
stone while the interior

was whitewashed with Bath stone arches, pillars and window quoins. The Revd Harold James Howden MA, was the vicar of Christ Church in 1931. He had been a Christian Missionary Society missionary in West China from 1905-27 and had his visiting cards printed in Chinese characters. Unexpectedly, the lavatory near the Vicar's Vestry proved to be of great value, being a rare and early example made by Doulton's of Lambeth. Doulton's used this lavatory in their 150th anniversary exhibition, and the church lost one of its more interesting items. In 1986 the church closed and in 1989 it was converted into luxury flats. You can see a crowded No. 27 tram going along Kew Road, which ran from Richmond to Kew via Kew Gardens.

THE TREES RATHER obscure the view of the former church, but apart from that the scene is remarkably unchanged today.

ST PETER'S CHURCH, PETERSHAM

ST PETER'S CHURCH dates back to Saxon times and is mentioned in the Domesday Book. It was rebuilt during the Georgian period and sadly only a small amount of the original church remains, namely the thirteenth-century chancel. Although it is quite a small

church, it has some beautiful original Georgian box pews (a rare survivor) and a very fine interior. At one time, the curacies of Petersham were joined with that of Kew and were not separated until 1885. It is possible to just see a few of the gravestones over the wall on the left-hand side of the image. Notice the solid, well-constructed gate leading to the path beyond the church, and the lovely old lamp set on the top of the pillar on the right.

ONLY ONE TREE now appears in the graveyard, whereas previously the view of the church was obscured by many. The semi-circular window on the side of the church is an unusual feature, and it can now be clearly seen. The path is frequently used by people going to the popular Petersham Nurseries and for those heading to the river.

93

RICHMOND LIME AND CEMENT COMPANY

DATING BACK TO the 1950s, this rare image shows the Richmond Lime and Cement
Company depot on Lion Road in Twickenham. The company lasted from 1934-97
and was initially managed by A.E. Balch and Frederick O. Maisey. It stocked plaster
(keene's and sirapite), bricks, tiles, slates, sinks, chimney pots, ridgings, fire bricks, fire clay,
sand, washed sand, ballast, lime and hair, mortar and putty. They were described as sanitary
specialists of every description.

THE DEPOT HAS been
replaced by Simba Court,
a block of residential flats.
The Lime and Cement
Company offices were
based in Water Lane, at
Ye Olde Feathers Yard.
The yard was thus named
as the offices were next to
an old antique shop called
Ye Olde Curiosity Shoppe.
The shop sold antique
furniture, porcelain,
jewellery and other items.

If you enjoyed this book, you may also be interested in …

Kingston upon Thames: Not a Guide to
SIMON WEBB

Did you know? For over a century, Kingston upon Thames was the de facto capital of England. Seven Saxon kings were crowned in the town. During the reign of Henry VIII, Hampton Court Palace featured bowling alleys, tennis courts and a 36,000 sq.ft kitchen. A Surrey market town, Kingston-upon-Thames is situated on the banks of the River Thames. This engaging little book explores both the modern life of this most vibrant and exciting of London boroughs, as well as its historical background.

978 0 7524 7968 2

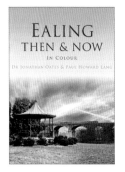

Ealing Then & Now
JONATHAN OATES & PAUL HOWARD LANG

Contrasting a selection of 45 archive images alongside full-colour modern photographs, this book traces some of the changes and developments that have taken place in Ealing during the last century. Accompanied by detailed and informative captions, these intriguing photographs reveal changing modes of fashion and transportation, shops and businesses, houses and public buildings, and, of course, some of the local people who once lived and worked in the area.

978 0 7524 6374 2

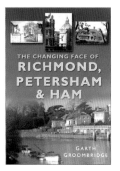

The Changing Face of Richmond, Petersham & Ham
GARTH GROOMBRIDGE

The Changing Face of Richmond, Petersham & Ham is a stroll through the author's recollections of a time now passed. Included here are a commentary on this historic area together with the photographs he took thirty to forty years ago, juxtaposed with images of how the places look today. From the changes made to the Richmond riverfront and shopping streets, to the comparatively unchanged area of The Green and the Hill, this book is sure to evoke memories for readers who know and love the area.

978 0 7509 4799 2

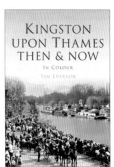

Kingston upon Thames Then & Now
TIM EVERSON

Kingston upon Thames Then & Now compares historical images of the area with modern photographs of the same viewpoints today. We can see just how much has changed and also what has survived the threats of war, demolition and redevelopment. A fascinating peak into the rich history of Kingston upon Thames, this book should be equally absorbing for those who know and love the area, and for those who love British history.

978 0 7524 7158 7

Visit our website and discover thousands of other History Press books.

www.thehistorypress.co.uk